PEACE AND PRAYER IN LIFE'S PANDEMICS and PANDEMONIUMS

SCRIPTURE PRAYER JOURNAL

Chaplain Karen Wilkins, BCC

ROYSTON
Publishing

BK Royston Publishing
P. O. Box 4321
Jeffersonville, IN 47131 | 502-802-5385
http://www.bkroystonpublishing.com
bkroystonpublishing@gmail.com

Cover Design: Elite Book Covers

Back Cover Photo Credit: LEZZO

ISBN-13: 978-1-955063-47-0

Printed in the United States of America

This book, Peace and Prayer in Life's Pandemics and Pandemoniums Scripture Prayer Journal, was birthed from my heart; a journal for those of whom I have served, supported, and encouraged throughout the COVID-19 pandemic. This scripture prayer journal was written for my family members, my friends, my colleagues at Inova Fairfax Hospital, the patients, and their family members. For all of those whom I have met in the various stages of my life this journal is for you too. This scripture prayer journal is for those of you who have been dealing with loss, grief, stress, worry, fear, and anxiety during life's pandemics and pandemoniums. I hope this scripture prayer journal will give you the peace of mind that you desire, and I hope that you allow peace to rule in your life and through your life.

This book has been strategically composed of various version of the bible that would amplify your understanding of peace and it has over 100 scriptures on peace that will assist you with a life of peacefulness; help you obtain peace of mind, help you with peace in your spirit, peace in your heart, and peace wherever you shall go. I hope throughout this journal you will discover the value in not only knowing your peace but being in full ownership over it. We talk about the power in owning materialistic things, rather it be our first home or our dream car, but what about the power in owning your own peace? By owning your peace, you become responsible for maintaining, cultivating and activating your peace in every situation. Do not allow peace antagonist to alter your state and disrupt the peace you have intended on possessing. You must be intentional when it comes to your peace because your peace begins with you.

I am reminded about a song that I heard when I was just a little girl; this song still resonates with me today. I share this song with you in hopes that it will also resonate with you too. Warren Cornell, who one day remained sitting in the large tent used for the meetings, after others had gone. Following a period of meditation, he jotted down some lines describing the peace of God in the heart of the believer.

Wonderful Peace

Peace, peace, wonderful peace
Coming down from the Father above
Sweep over my spirit forever, I pray In fathomless billows of love!

What a treasure I have in this wonderful peace,
Buried deep in the heart of my soul,
So secure that no power can mine it away,
While the years of eternity roll!

I am resting tonight in this wonderful peace,
Resting sweetly in Jesus' control;
For I'm kept from all danger by night and by day,
And His glory is flooding my soul!

(Words: Warren D. Cornell and William G. Cooper, 1889. MUSIC: W. G. C., 1889. Public Domain.)

This book is dedicated

To my three sons Kevin, Jeffery, and Blake: May the peace of God rest, rule and abide in your life now and forever.

I also dedicate this book to my grandchildren, whom I love dearly. My mother, Willie Mae House, whose love, has no bounds and even as the year goes I have never missed a birthday card from her. My sister, Robin Ellis, who's support spans across decades to me and my children. My two brothers, Kirk and Bryan, and all my nieces, nephews and great nieces and nephews, who reminds me constantly that there is a generation I'm laying the ground work for. I pray that God's perfect peace be with you every day, in every way and everywhere you go take the peace of God with you. My love for you all is immeasurable and I am grateful for the village that surrounds me, my continued fervent prayers are with you all.

Special Dedication to the House family, Ellis family, and Wilkins family I love you all more than you know. My thoughts of prayer, peace, and love are never far off. Grace and Peace be multiplied to each and every one of you!

Contributors

I would be remiss if I didn't take the opportunity to acknowledge the contributions of 'The Mothers in Zion'. They are key figures on the journey of Releasing the Word International Prayer Call (RTWIPC), their impact on the ministry and my life has no boundary. Connected by our home state of California, it was their dedication to the ministry, love of Christ and prayers that availeth much that solidified the relationship. Their words of wisdom, knowledge, peace, and prayer have planted deep seeds in my life and in the life of others. The seeds that they have sown continue to germinate. I truly appreciate and thank God for my cousin, Evangelist Virginia Riley who connected me and the ministry to these amazing Mothers of Zion. Many of times we fail to give the appropriate flowers to those still living, those who have impacted our lives for the better. I must in this moment give them the appropriate honor for the impact these mothers have had on the many lives they have touched. I understand the importance of cherishing the scriptures, words, gifts, stories and recipes of those who were born before me and I want to be sure to captivate the tangible experiences these women have with their walk with God. It was important to me that I utilize 'The Mothers in Zion'. These mothers have great wisdom and knowledge and said, 'yes' to sharing the word of God on peace and prayer in life's pandemics on Monday nights. These mothers' words were so powerful, encouraging and full of wisdom. Their words had so much impact on our lives that I wanted to record a snippet of the seeds that they sowed into our lives. This is part of the legacy that these Mothers in Zion would leave for us should they leave this world before us.

Pastor Emeritus Dr. Lelia Edwards, Miracle Temple Apostolic Pentecostal Church, Richmond, CA

Philippians 2:5 (KJV) Let this mind be in you, which was also in Christ Jesus:

Philippians 4:7 (KJV) And the peace of God, which passeth all understanding, shall keep your hearts and minds through Christ Jesus.

We let the devil get in our face and take our peace because we don't know who we are and whose we are. Always remember this is not the first plague in this world; there was one in Egypt. We are living in the last day and we can wake up to anything anyway. God is in control of this world; he loved the world, and he died for this world. I want to encourage the saints to read your Bible because in the scriptures you will find everything that you need to walk with the Lord. There are principles that produce peace. You can't just say, "I want peace and peace is coming, but there are conditions." Let this mind be in you that is also in Christ Jesus: we have to have God's mind. In troubled times, like this pandemic, we must know how to process the peace of God. John 14:27 says (paraphrased), "Peace I leave with you, my peace I give to you and not as the world gives. Don't let your heart be afraid. God is going to take care of you, he always has and he always will." You can't let peace rule if you don't have peace. We need to go back to the altar and get another dip so that we can obtain peace. We are called to the gospel of peace. Don't let the devil upset you. God gives us peace because he is the Prince of Peace. If you obey God, he will bless you going in and going out.

Mother Martha Womack, Bethesda Apostolic Faith Church, Merced, CA

Philippians 4:6–7 (KJV) Be careful for nothing; but in everything by prayer and supplication with thanksgiving let your requests be made known unto God. And the peace of God, which passeth all understanding, shall keep your hearts and minds through Christ Jesus.

Luke 18:1 (KJV) And he spake a parable unto them to this end, that men ought always to pray, and not to faint.

Isaiah 26:3 (KJV) Thou wilt keep him in perfect peace, whose mind is stayed on thee: because he trusteth in thee.

(Meaning of peace that that was researched) 1 Peace is freedom from disquieting or oppressive thoughts or emotions. Right now there are a lot of emotions running rampant in the land because all the things that is going on right now. 2, a realm where chaos is not allowed to enter; 3, inner tranquility based on peace with God. God will keep us in peace if we let him. Anyone can have peace as long as it's not being challenged; your faith has to stand strong and trust God. You have peace with God because you have faith. Peace and faith work together. These are the last days and evil is all around us. We don't know when our faith will be challenged. Daniel had peace because he always prayed. He prayed three times a day. He will keep you in perfect peace, meaning there is no lack in your peace. Daniel had peace even when he went into the lion's den. He wasn't angry. God goes before us and prepares the way before us if we let him. God took care of Daniel because of his faith and trust in God. We have a God who will fight our battles. God is always with us, and he will keep us if we keep our mind on him. We can get all upset and allow our peace to be disturbed, but we can't allow our peace to be disturbed; we have to trust God—he can do what no other can do.

Mother Joyce Penn, Miracle Temple Apostolic Pentecostal Church, Richmond, CA

Psalms 4:8 (KJV) I will both lay me down in peace, and sleep: for thou, Lord, only makest me dwell in safety.

Psalms 19:14 (KJV) Let the words of my mouth, and the meditation of my heart, be acceptable in thy sight, O Lord, my strength, and my redeemer.

We can meditate on positive things, or we can meditate on negative things. Meditations are what the heart precedes. The Lord is my strength; my desire is that everything that comes forth from me will be acceptable in his sight. The fact that he is my strength, I never lose track of: he is the only eternal redeemer for those who seek eternal life with him. Hold your peace during the pandemic; keep your faith. He lays us down in peace. I will keep you in perfect peace whose mind stands firm on him. Perfect peace means that you are not worried about what happens around you. Perfect means without any fault, God takes care of his people.

Mother Evelyn Harris, Bethesda Apostolic Church, Fresno, CA

Psalms 57:1–2 (KJV) Be merciful unto me, O God, be merciful unto me: for my soul trusteth in thee: yea, in the shadow of thy wings will I make my refuge, until these calamities be overpast. I will cry unto God most high; unto God that performeth all things for me.

Keep in mind the peace that only God can bring you, the peace of the almighty God. This crisis that we are in is new to us, but there is nothing new under the sun. There is a panic in the air, but don't forget to get into a quiet place and listen to the voice of God. I'm 80 years old, and through my lifetime I have seen emergencies, and I've seen some things that put fear in the hearts of people, but my go-to has always been word of God; that was my peace. We have to realize our peace will always remain with God. We must fear the Lord more than this pandemic. Anxiety causes stress and confusion and causes us to get distracted from where God wants us to go hold on. God is trying to get our attention. We are sheltering in place, and now we have to be still in our home. We have to face issues that have evaded us. Do a self-examination during this pandemic. Remember God's promises and know that they are true. We have a God that is greater than the pandemic. Do not succumb to the wiles of the enemy. He is a liar and a cheat. I am to pray fast and walk by faith. I'm thinking God and praising him and I don't think about the pandemic or fear. You are filling yourself with joy and peace of the Lord.

Mother Rosetta Griggs, True Life Worship Center, Stockton, CA

Psalms 4:8 (KJV) I will both lay me down in peace, and sleep: for thou, Lord, only makest me dwell in safety.

Psalms 119:164–165 (KJV) Seven times a day do I praise thee because of thy righteous judgments. Great peace have they which love thy law: and nothing shall offend them.

Psalms 119:165 (NIV) Great peace have those who love your law, and nothing can make them stumble.

Nehemiah said, "I am doing a great work, so I can't come down. Why should I come down?" This nation needs people on the wall prayer. Without the peace giver there is no peace; unless you know him, there is no peace. Peace is a state of quiet, not speaking, silence, not easily excited or disturbed, and resting in God. David said two things: I'm going to lie down and sleep. I know that the Lord is watching over me and keeping me safe. I'm not going to worry about it. I am going to put it in God's hands and let him take care of the situation. God is able to do abundantly; we just need to trust him. He will bring us out. In the Old Testament, it says that peace means completeness, no lack—it's full; it speaks of soundness, sound mind and sound body. Get the word of God in you and rise in you. David prayed to God seven times a day. Pray without ceasing; keep a prayer going on at all times and the Lord will see you through the most difficult times. Peace is God given. Great peace that loves thy law and nothing shall offend thee. God is able to give us peace today. No matter what you are going through today, God is with you. The New Testament says that peace often refers to inner tranquility, and poise of the saints who trust is in God through Christ. Now poise should be humbleness of mind and spirit waiting on the Lord. Our trust should be in God through Christ. Peace I leave with you. I'm leaving you with a gift. Don't be troubled and don't be afraid. I'm leaving you with peace. This peace will calm trouble minds.

The Effective Use Of This Scripture Prayer Journal

Each scripture and prayer is designed to offer you thought provoking revelation on the power of peace; as well as enhance your knowledge and understanding on the importance of maintaining your peace. Please take your time and read each scripture carefully so that you can get an understanding of God's word. This will also allow the words to get engrafted into your life and become part of your everyday living. You may need to revisit each prayer and scripture in order to connect with your inner peace. You can use this journal at your own pace. You can start reading and writing in the beginning, in middle, or the end of this journal. You have additional space to write your thoughts and feelings. As you begin to journal, I pray that peace will be your portion.

The main scripture theme for this prayer journal book

Listed below are scriptures from various versions in the book of Philippians 4:6–9. Paul wrote these scriptures as part of a letter to the people in Philippi to uplift and encourage them. I hope these scriptures will inspire you to change your mindset and restore peace back into your life.

Philippians 4:6–9 NLT

6 Don't worry about anything; instead, pray about everything. Tell God what you need, and thank him for all he has done. 7 Then you will experience God's peace, which exceeds anything we can understand. His peace will guard your hearts and minds as you live in Christ Jesus. 8 And now, dear brothers and sisters, one final thing. Fix your thoughts on what is true, and honorable, and right, and pure, and lovely, and admirable. Think about things that are excellent and worthy of praise. 9 Keep putting into practice all you learned and received from me—everything you heard from me and saw me doing. Then the God of peace will be with you.

Philippians 4:6–9 AMP

6 Do not be anxious *or* worried about anything, but in everything [every circumstance and situation] by prayer and petition with thanksgiving, continue to make your [specific] requests known to God. 7 And the peace of God [that peace which reassures the heart, that peace] which transcends all understanding, [that peace which] stands guard over your hearts and your minds in Christ Jesus [is yours]. 8 Finally, believers, whatever is true, whatever is honorable *and* worthy of respect, whatever is right *and* confirmed by God's word, whatever is pure *and* wholesome, whatever is lovely *and* brings peace, whatever is admirable *and* of good repute; if there is any excellence, if there is anything worthy of praise, think *continually* on these things [center your mind on them, and implant them in your heart]. 9 The things which you have learned and received and heard and seen in me, practice these things [in daily life], and the God [who is the source] of peace *and* well-being will be with you.

Philippians 4:6-9 MSG

6-7 Don't fret or worry. Instead of worrying, pray. Let petitions and praises shape your worries into prayers, letting God know your concerns. Before you know it, a sense of God's wholeness, everything coming together for good, will come and settle you down. It's wonderful what happens when Christ displaces worry at the center of your life. 8-9 Summing it all up, friends, I'd say you'll do best by filling your minds and meditating on things true, noble, reputable, authentic, compelling, gracious—the best, not the worst; the beautiful, not the ugly; things to praise, not things to curse. Put into practice what you learned from me, what you heard and saw and realized. Do that, and God, who makes everything work together, will work you into his most excellent harmonies.

Exodus 14:14 KJV

"The LORD shall fight for you, and ye shall hold your peace."

Today's Prayer:

Dear God,

I honor you today and I thank you for your protection and peace every day in every way. I thank you because your word tells me, _____, [your name] to hold my peace because you will fight for me. I can always count on you to fight on my behalf. I don't have to fight in the battles that life brings and in the situations that I face every day because I can rest in knowing that you will fight for me in every way and every day. I am grateful for your peace, peace that you bring, peace that you give. God, again, I thank you in advance for fighting for me and giving me peace of mind. Amen.

_____

_____

_____

_____

_____

_____

_____

_____

_____

Leviticus 26:6 NLT

"I will give you peace in the land, and you will be able to sleep with no cause for fear."

Today's Prayer:

Lord God,

I thank you today for your peace, the peace that only you can give me. I thank you for peace in my life, in my home, in my marriage, in my family, on my job, and in my mind. Oh, yes, it is your peace, peace like no other. Your peace keeps me from all fear. You are my peace and that peace only comes from you. I also thank you because you allow me to sleep and rest in green pastures without any fear, without any worry, and without any anxiety. I am thankful today that I have your peace and that your peace causes me not to fear. I can have tranquility and serenity and be restored because of the peace of God.

_____

_____

_____

_____

_____

_____

_____

Numbers 6:26 AMP

"The LORD lift up His countenance (face) upon you [with divine approval] And give you peace [a tranquil heart and life]."

Today's Prayer:

Father God,

I thank you for allowing your face to shine upon me and with your approval; you have given me that tranquility of peace in the midst of all that life brings me. I still have your peace. I have your divine approval of peace and that is all I need. When things get chaotic, when life seems a little crazy and in the midst of crisis, you have given me your divine approval that I will have peace I can rest in your peace, peace like no other. The peace of God that keeps me in Christ Jesus, it is that inner peace that only comes from you. I am grateful to you God, for your peace that gives me serenity in my heart and in my mind. I accept your gift of peace.

Numbers 25:12 ASV

"Wherefore say, Behold, I give unto him my covenant of peace."

Today's Prayer:

Dear God,

I thank you because those who came before me were given an agreement of your peace and therefore I can be a partaker of that same agreement, your promise of peace that you give to me in every way; it is your peace. It's all because of you that I can have peace and be peaceful in all that I say and in all that I do. I can take your peace with me everywhere I go and in every situation I face. Your peace is my lifeline and I can't live without your peace. Peace, peace wonderful peace. I thank you for your covenant of peace. Amen.

_____

_____

_____

_____

_____

_____

_____

_____

Judges 6:23-24 AMP

"The LORD said to him, "Peace to you, do not be afraid; you shall not die." Then Gideon built an altar there to the LORD and named it The LORD is Peace."

Today's Prayer:

Dear Lord God,

Thank you for being my peace in every situation and in every circumstance. Even when faced with fear and death you told me not to be afraid. I can profess that you have guaranteed that I will not die. Lord God, show me a place to build an altar in my home or wherever I am and call that place, the Lord of Peace. I want to be able to go to that place and obtain your favor and peace. That is the place where I can feel your peace when life is raging all around me. That is the place where I can command that peace be still. That is the place of tranquility and peacefulness. Thank you God for your peace, it's that perfect peace where fear, worry and anxiety can't penetrate because it is your peace. I am safe in your peaceful arms. Amen.

_____

_____

_____

_____

_____

_____

_____

Judges 18:6 NLV

The religious leader said to them, "Go in peace. The way you are going is pleasing to the Lord."

Today's Prayer:

Dear Heavenly Father,

When I depart from a place and a situation I want to hear you say, "Go in peace," and I want the direction that I'm going to be pleasing to you. My desire is that my ways please you. I want my life to please you and everything that I do; I want it to be pleasing to you. And my desire is to hear you say, "The way you are going is pleasing to the Lord." Allow me to hear those words that can only come from you. I want the words that come out of my mouth to be pleasing to you, I want my hands to please you, I want my feet to please you, I want my eyes to please you, I want my ears to please you, and I want my whole being to please you and to be at peace in every way and every day. Thank you, Father, for your perfect peace, peace like no other. Amen.

1 Samuel 25:6 NLV

"Say to him, 'Have a long life. Peace be to you. Peace be to your family. And peace be to all that you have.'"

Today's Prayer:

Ah God,

You are awesome in all your ways and for that I say, "thank you." I thank you for the long life that you will give me and for allowing peace to be with me, _____, [your name] in every way and every minute of the day. I thank you for the joy of having peace in my heart, peace in my mind, peace in my spirit, peace in my family, peace in relationships with my family members and friends, peace on my job, peace at the grocery store, peace at the mall, and peace at the bank. I thank you for giving me peace everywhere I go and peace in all that I do. Father God, you give me peace in my comings and goings and for that I say, "thank you." I can't thank you enough for your gift of peace. You are the only one who can give me this type of peace and for that I say, "thank you." God I thank you for your peace, peace in all that I have. Your perfect peace is all that I need. Amen.

_____

_____

_____

_____

_____

_____

_____

Job 13:5 KJV

"O that ye would altogether hold your peace! and it should be your wisdom."

Today's Prayer:

Lord God,

Thank you for your son, Jesus Christ. He is still a great example of your peace and calm. In all that he endured, he maintained a sense calm and peacefulness. Help me today to hold my peace even when I feel like I've been treated indifferently. If I hold my peace, it should be my wisdom. The wisdom that comes from holding my peace is what I desire to obtain in order to make the right decisions and say the right things at the right time. Lord, it's in your peacefulness and tranquility where I find your wisdom and knowledge. Thank you for your peace, the peace that I can rest in. Amen.

_____

_____

_____

_____

_____

_____

_____

Job 33:31 KJV

"Mark well, O Job, hearken unto me: hold thy peace, and I will speak."

Today's Prayer:

Dear Father God,

Job exemplifies a wonderful example for me of what one of your peace projects looks like. Lord, now allow me to be the splitting image of your peace. Lord let me hear your words when you say, hear me, _____, (put your name in that space): hold your peace and you will speak for me. My Lord, You are showing me every day and in every circumstance that I don't have to say a word. If I hold my peace and stay quiet, then you will speak for me. Help me to trust your words and be still; know that you will speak up on my behalf. I know that everything that Job went through, he didn't go through for not but you God compensated him. He did not lose everything because you gave him back those things that he lost. God, I thank you for your peace and quietness because it is possible not to say a word knowing that you will speak for me.

_____

_____

_____

_____

_____

_____

_____

Job 33:33 AMPC

"If [you do] not [have anything to say], listen to me; hold your peace, and I will teach you wisdom."

Today's Prayer:

Lord God,

Teach me your ways; teach me to say nothing when I have nothing good or positive to say. Allow me to listen for your voice and your words when you say, "Hold Your Peace." I pray today that my flesh falls under your command. I want you to teach me your way and teach me your wisdom. Lord God, teach me to listen to you and to hold my peace in the midst of all that I have to endure. I know that there will be times where I will not hit the mark regarding peace but I'm learning that things come up in my life to break my peace. Help me to recognize those things and maintain the peace that you gave to me. Thank you, God, for helping me to hold my words and be quiet while you are teach me some valuables lessons in being peaceful. Amen.

_____

_____

_____

_____

_____

_____

_____

Psalm 4:8 AMP

"In peace [and with a tranquil heart] I will both lie down and sleep, For You alone, O Lᴏʀᴅ, make me dwell in safety *and* confident trust."

Today's Prayer:

Lord God,

As I rest in the peace of your comfort and in your loving presence, I take joy knowing you are with me and you have taken care of every one of my concerns. You make me rest and feel secure in your protection and assurance. I have no fear because I am safe with you. Because of your peace and tranquil heart, I can lie down without fear and worry because I feel safe, and I am confident in who you are in my life. Thank you for your peace. In Jesus' Name, Amen.

Psalm 29:11 AMP

"The LORD will give [unyielding and impenetrable] strength to His people; The LORD will bless His people with peace."

Today's Prayer:

Father God,

I thank you for giving me your solid and impossible to understand strength and peace during the most difficult times in my life. You are my strength, strength like no other. I thank you for the bond that we share. You are with me and I am with you because of that, you will bless me with your peace. I am grateful that your blessings fall in many forms and your peace is what I need today. I can't buy your peace but because of the relationship I have with you, I can obtain your peace. I praise you for the peace of God that I have. Thank you. Amen.

_____

_____

_____

_____

_____

_____

_____

_____

Psalm 34:14 MSG

"Turn your back on sin; do something good. Embrace peace—don't let it get away!"

Today's Prayer:

Dear God,

Today is a good day to turn my back on everything that hinders me and everything that keeps me from drawing closer to you. I, _____, [your name] will turn away from sin and do well by embracing your peace. I will not let my peace get away from me. I will maintain and cultivate my peace. It belongs to me, it's mine, and I will take ownership of the peace that you have blessed me with. I will not allow anyone to take my peace. I declare today that peace breakers move out from among me: you are not welcome into this space of peacefulness. God I thank you for my peace. That place that is peaceful in every way—it belongs to me.

_____

_____

_____

_____

_____

_____

_____

_____

_____

Psalm 37:11 TLB

"But all who humble themselves before the Lord shall be given every blessing and shall have wonderful peace."

Today's Prayer:

Lord God,

I thank you today for your blessed promises that you gave me in your word. You promised me, _____, [your name] that if I humble myself, then I am available for every blessing that you have for me, and the bonus is you guaranteed me that I will have your perfect peace. I'm grateful for your wonderful peace that is obtainable through faith, your precious word, and the covenant that I have with you. Lord God, I receive all that you have for me, especially your peace. Peace in my heart and in my mind. I will let peace rule. Thank you. Amen.

_____

_____

_____

_____

_____

_____

_____

Psalm 37:37 TLB

"But the good man—what a different story! For the good man—the blameless, the upright, the man of peace—he has a wonderful future ahead of him. For him there is a happy ending."

Today's Prayer:

Gracious and Heavenly Father,

I am thankful and pleased that there is a wonderful future for me, _____, [your name] no matter what my story is and how it ends. For a good man, for a good woman, and for the one who is of peace, there is a happy ending. Thank you Father for your word that reassurance me of the importance of being upright and peaceful. Your word continues to remind me of my outcome in all that I face and endure. As long as I am blameless, upright, and peaceful, there's a wonderful future and a blissful ending for me. Oh Father God, I look forward to that day. Thank you for you peacefulness. Amen.

_____

_____

_____

_____

_____

_____

_____

Psalms 85:8 NLT

"I listen carefully to what God the LORD is saying, for he speaks peace to his faithful people. But let them not return to their foolish ways."

Today's Prayer:

Most Holy and Gracious God,

Help me to listen carefully to your words and take all that you say in consideration. When I'm in the midst of turmoil, chaos, and crisis you are speaking peace to me, _____, [your name] in every way. Father God, please don't allow me to ever turn back to my foolish ways, when you have offered me your wonderful, perfect, and unyielding peace. It is your peace that keeps me calm when everything around me says I should be afraid, worried, and scared. I wear your peace and I take it with me everywhere I go. Peace, peace wonderful peace. I thank you, God, for your peace. Amen.

Psalms 85:10 NLT

"Unfailing love and truth have met together. Righteousness and peace have kissed!"

Today's Prayer:

Ah God,

I can breathe and go on with my daily life because of your peace. Thank you for your goodness and mercy. Your unfailing love for me, _____, [your name] and truth have collided together and have empowered me to strive to live in right standing with you. I'm grateful to you, God that your righteousness and peace have embraced and kissed. I am determined to live a life that is whole in order to maintain and embrace your peace. God, I thank you for your righteousness and your peace. In Jesus' Name, Amen.

_____

_____

_____

_____

_____

_____

_____

_____

_____

_____

_____

_____

Psalms 119:165 NLT

"Those who love your instructions have great peace and do not stumble."

Today's Prayer:

Good Morning God,

Thank you for your awesomeness and your spoken word that gives me great peace. It's because of your peace that you give to me that nothing is able to offend me. You make me lie down in green pastures and nothing shall disturb my peace. In the midnight hour, nothing shall disturb my peace. The wee hours in the morning phone calls will not disturb my peace. I know that some things happen in life to distract me and disturb my peace, but I will not be moved because you gave me the gift of peace. The peace that only you can give me, _____, [your name] surrounds me in all that I do. Thank you so much, God, for the spirit of peacefulness. Your peace gives me unlimited joy. I will embrace your peace this day forward. Amen.

_____

_____

_____

_____

_____

_____

_____

_____

_____

Psalms 120:7 MSG

"I'm all for peace, but the minute I tell them so, they go to war!"

Today's Prayer:

Lord God,

Help me, _____, [your name] to know when they are for war that I remain peaceful. Allow me to sustain in the atmosphere of peace when chaos is all around me. Help me to go in peace, and when I leave, help me to leave in peace. God I want to be in the place where your peace resides. I don't want to move out of the place of your peace, but keep me when the storms of life are raging about me. Help me to grab a hold of your soothing peace and calmness that can change the situation and the atmosphere all around me. Thank you for your covenant keeping peace. Amen.

_____

_____

_____

_____

_____

_____

_____

_____

_____

_____

_____

Psalms 122:8 NLB

"I will now say, "May peace be within you," for the good of my brothers and my friends."

Today's Prayer:

Dear Gracious and Most High God,

Let your peace be within me, around me, under me, in front of me, and behind me. The peace of God that surrounds me is for me as well as for the benefit of all those whom I come in contact with. The peace that dwells in me will bring others this same peace; it is your peace that we all need in every way. Right now I dispatch your peace, the peace of God to all who are in need of peace. Allow your peace to rest, rule, and abide in the lives of those feeling restless. Thank you God, Amen.

_____

_____

_____

_____

_____

_____

_____

_____

_____

_____

_____

Proverbs 12:20 NLV

"Lying is in the heart of those who plan what is bad, but those who plan peace have joy."

Today's Prayer:

My Father, My God,

No matter who lies and no matter who schemes up evil devices against me and others, allow me, _____, [your name] to plan peace. I want to be peaceful in all that I do and say, not so I can just have joy but because I want to be peaceful. I want to remain in a peaceful state of mind. I want to share your peace with others and let them feel your peacefulness. God, you are the epitome of peace: allow me to mirror that same peace in all that I do, in all that I say and wherever I go allow your peace to follow me. I am made in your image and after your likeness, and I must inhabit your peace. God, I just want to thank you for your peace and joy that you have given to me.

_____

_____

_____

_____

_____

_____

_____

_____

_____

_____

Proverbs 16:7 NLV

"When the ways of a man are pleasing to the Lord, He makes even those who hate him to be at peace with him."

Proverbs 16:7 NLT

"When people's lives please the LORD, even their enemies are at peace with them."

Today's Prayer:

Lord,

Allow my ways to please you in all that I say and in all that I do because those who hate me will be at peace with me. I want you to approve of my life where my enemies will shake my hand and be peaceful with me. I want peace everywhere my feet tread, and I want that same peace to follow me. Lord God, thank you for being the God of peace and for giving me the peace that I will never understand. God, it's your peace that leaves me speechless in the midst of trauma and in the midst of the tears. Your unyielding peace surrounds me and for that I say thank you. Amen.

_____

_____

_____

_____

_____

Proverbs 17:28 AMP

"Even a [callous, arrogant] fool, when he keeps silent, is considered wise; When he closes his lips he is regarded as sensible (prudent, discreet) *and* a man of understanding."

Today's Prayer:

Oh Precious Father,

If a fool can keep his silence allow me, _____, [your name] to be considered wise by staying quiet when my flesh wants to rise up. Allow me to be a person who is discreet and understanding by closing my lips and remaining peaceful. I don't have to have the first word or the last word. I need to remain peaceful. Help me to trust you because you said if I will be still and quiet that you will fight for me. I just need to hold back my words and let you do the work. Thank you for your promises of peace. Amen.

_____

_____

_____

_____

_____

_____

_____

_____

Ecclesiastes 3:8 MSG

"A right time to wage war and another to make peace."

Today's Prayer:

God! Oh Holy One,

I thank you for your words that tell me that I must make peace even if I'm in the atmosphere of war. It's your peace that will calm the environment that I'm in and bring in the spirit of tranquility and peacefulness. It is up to me to make peace with everybody in every way. God, I thank you for your peace that goes beyond my understanding; only your peace can do this. It's peace like no other. Amen.

Isaiah 9:6 KJV

"His name shall be called Wonderful, Counsellor, The mighty God, The everlasting Father, The Prince of Peace."

Today's Prayer:

Oh Mighty God, The Everlasting Father,

I can rest assured that you are my *Prince of Peace*. You lead the way in peacefulness and you are the head of my peace. You are so gracious to make a covenant with me and to share your peace with me. Thank you for being the *Prince of Peace* that continues to work and rule in my life. It's your peace that keeps me in the right frame of mind when life is raging all around me. Thank you, God, for you have allowed *The Prince of Peace* to reign forevermore in and around me.

_____

_____

_____

_____

_____

_____

_____

_____

_____

Isaiah 26:3 AMP

"You will keep in perfect *and* constant peace *the one* whose mind is steadfast [that is, committed and focused on You—in both inclination and character], Because he trusts *and* takes refuge in You [with hope and confident expectation]."

Today's Prayer:

Dear God,

You said that you will keep me in perfect peace whose mind is committed and focused on you. This means that no matter what I go through or what I have to face if I keep my mind on you, you will keep me, _____, [your name] in your continual perfect peace. Lord God, I trust you, and I take refuge in you. I have great expectations, and I have confidence in you, and I know that your peace will reside within me and through me. I love you, God, and I thank you for your peace, peace like no other. Amen.

_____

_____

_____

_____

_____

_____

_____

_____

Isaiah 26:12 AMP

"LORD, You will establish peace for us, Since You have also performed for us all that we have done."

Today's Prayer:

Lord,

You are awesome in all of your ways. You will create and form your peace for me and in me. You have done so much more for me. I can't begin to name all that you've performed in my life and in the lives of those around me. I just want to thank you for your peace, peace that I need in all that I do, in all that I say, and everywhere I go. Thank you so much for this peaceful state of mind that you have executed in my life. Amen.

Isaiah 32:17 NLV

"The work of being right and good will give peace. From the right and good work will come quiet trust forever."

Today's Prayer:

Father God,

Help me to be in right standing with you and do your good work that will bring me peace. My prayer is that the work that I do will bring quietness and long-lasting trust. Thank you, God, for your goodness and mercy and your loving kindness that is better than life itself. Lord I thank you so much for your peace, that is the peace that is unquestionable but yet I can't understand because it's your peace. You are the source of my peace. Thank you. Amen.

_____

_____

_____

_____

_____

_____

_____

_____

_____

Isaiah 45:7 AMP

"The One forming light and creating darkness, Causing peace and creating disaster; I am the LORD who does all these things."

Today's Prayer:

Dear God,

The one who created the Heaven and Earth, you called the light and the darkness into place, and you created peace for me in the midst of the storm and life crisis. You are the Lord who does great and mighty things and there is nothing that you can't do. Thank you for your covenant of peace. Amen.

_____

_____

_____

_____

_____

_____

_____

_____

_____

_____

Isaiah 48:22 NLT

"But there is no peace for the wicked," says the LORD."

Today's Prayer:

Lord God,

I thank you for your peace and love. There is no peace for the wicked, but I thank you for the peace that you've given to me. It's your perfect love that casts out all fear and gives me peace. Peace and fear can't reside together so I, _____, [your name] declare and decree your peace over every situation today that I have to face. In The Name of Our Lord and Savior Jesus Christ, I thank you for your gift of peace, peace that is calm and still. Amen.

_____

_____

_____

_____

_____

_____

_____

_____

_____

_____

Isaiah 53:5 KJV

"But he was wounded for our transgressions, he was bruised for our iniquities: the chastisement of our peace was upon him; and with his stripes we are healed."

Today's Prayer:

Dear Jesus,

I thank you for being wounded for all my wrongdoings and for being bruised for all my sins. You took rebuke, punishment, and discipline so that I can have your perfect peace. Every stripe that you took and endured was for me, _____, [your name] so that I can be healed from every disease, sickness, and illness. Thank you for all you've done for me and for giving me peace like no other. Amen.

_____

_____

_____

_____

_____

_____

_____

_____

_____

Isaiah 54:10 MSG

"For even if the mountains walk away and the hills fall to pieces, My love won't walk away from you, my covenant commitment of peace won't fall apart. The GOD who has compassion on you says so."

Today's Prayer:

Dear Most Holy and Sovereign God,

I, _____, [your name] can rest assured on your word, that even though people may walk away from me and my world may seem to be crushing in on me and falling to pieces, you will never leave me nor will you forsake me. Your peace will always be with me because you told me, peace I leave with you. You gave me a promise and commitment of your peace that will not fall apart when everything in my life seems to. Thank you for your compassion and your covenant of Peace that rest upon my life. Amen.

_____

_____

_____

_____

_____

_____

_____

_____

Isaiah 57:2 AMP

"He enters into peace [through death]; They rest in their beds (graves), *Each one* who walked uprightly [following God's will, living with integrity]."

Today's Prayer:

Most Holy and Gracious God,

Thank you for your sweet peace that I can rest in; you promised me peace on earth and peace in death. When I die, I know that I will go to my eternal resting place in peace because of my honest walk with you and living a life of integrity. I may live in a world where there is chaos all around, but you have promised me your peace. I will continue with your peace in life and death. Thank you, Father, for you peace. Amen.

Isaiah 57:19 TLB

"Peace, peace to them, both near and far, for I will heal them all."

Today's Prayer:

Lord God,

Thank you for your peace, that unexplainable peace that you've offered to me that is near and far. No matter where I go, I know that your peace will be there with me and around me. I thank you, God, for your healing power that your peace brings me. When fear arises, your peace overcomes my fear and worry. Your peace places me in a state of calmness and tranquility. Peace, Peace wonderful peace. There is no peace like the peace of God. Thank you, God for your peace. Amen.

_____

_____

_____

_____

_____

_____

_____

_____

_____

Isaiah 57:21 AMP

"There is no peace," says my God, "for the wicked."

Today's Prayer:

Dear God,

I thank you because no matter what happens in my life concerning injustice, I can rest assured that your right hand of power will bring justice. There is peace for me, but for those who bring on wicked devices there is no peace for them. I don't have to worry about getting even or trying to get back at anyone because you have given me a precious gift called peace. Even when the storms of life are raging, I have your peace. In the midst of crisis, I have your peace. When death is all around me, I have your peace, but those who are evil have no peace. God, I thank you for your peace, Amen.

_____

_____

_____

_____

_____

_____

_____

_____

_____

Jeremiah 29:11 KJV

"For I know the thoughts that I think toward you, saith the LORD, thoughts of peace, and not of evil, to give you an expected end."

Today's Prayer:

Lord God,

Thank you for the thoughts that you think of me, _____, [your name] your thoughts of peace and not of evil. Thank you for the thoughts toward me that you think are to give me an anticipated end. I am so grateful that when you think of me, you think of peace concerning me. Peace like no other, peace that calms all my concerns and the peace that I need every day. Thank you God for your peacefulness in my life, that means so much to me. Amen.

_____

_____

_____

_____

_____

_____

_____

_____

_____

Jeremiah 33:6 NLV

"See, I will make it well again, and I will heal them. I will let them have much peace and truth."

Today's Prayer:

Lord,

As you promise others restoration and healing, I am overjoyed that I can also be a partaker of those things, as well. I thank you for much peace and truth that you so freely give. Your covenant of peace shall abide with me, in me, around me, and through me. Lord, I Thank you, for your unbreakable peace that is with me always. Amen.

Ezekiel 37:26 AMP

"I will make a covenant of peace with them; it will be an everlasting covenant with them. And I will place them and multiply them, and will put My sanctuary in their midst forever."

Today's Prayer:

Lord,

I thank you for making a peace agreement with me and an everlasting promise of your peace. You are a refuge in my life forever and for that I say thank you. Lord, you have always been there when times were tough because of your covenant of peace that you made with me. You have become a sanctuary in the midst of my life forever, and I am so grateful that I have you in my life. Thank you for your peace, peace that calms me in the midst of life's storms. Amen.

Haggai 2:9 NLV

"'This house will be even greater than it was before,' says the Lord of All. 'And in this place I will give peace,' says the Lord of All."

Today's Prayer:

Lord,

Thank you so much for allowing me to know that my house will be even greater than before because of your peace. Even in the midst of chaos and craziness, your word gives me a peace assurance of this. I trust your word because you said it. You are great and mighty. I thank you Father for giving me, _____, [your name] your peace, your ultimate, and your divine peace. Your peace is like nothing else. Amen.

_____

_____

_____

_____

_____

_____

_____

_____

Zechariah 8:16 TLB

"Here is your part: Tell the truth. Be fair. Live at peace with everyone."

Today's Prayer:

Oh Mighty God and Loving Father,

You are great and loving, and you've given me my own part to do in this world and that is to tell the truth, be fair, and live in peace with everyone. Thank you for sharing your word with me and giving me an assignment that is not far-fetched. It's possible to be honest, open-minded, and live in peace with everyone. Your peace that you give is a gift to me that I will cherish and unwrap your perfect gift of peace. Thank you God, for your gift of peace, peace in every way.

_____

_____

_____

_____

_____

_____

_____

_____

_____

Matthew 5:9 AMP

"Blessed [spiritually calm with life-joy in God's favor] are the makers *and* maintainers of peace, for they will [express His character and] be called the sons of God."

Today's Prayer:

Most Holy and Loving God

Thank you for your word and your promises that you made to me about being a peacemaker and one that will maintain your peace. Allow me _____, [your name] to be a peacemaker and maintain peace so that I can express your character. I thank you that I am called the son/daughter of God. Your words give me the confidence that I need to obtain your perfect peace, pursue your peace, and maintain your peace. Your word tells me that blessed are the makers who maintain peace that they will be called the sons/daughters of God. I thank you, God, for your peace, peace like no other, peace that you give to those who walk closely with you. Thank you for peace in my mind and spirit. Amen.

_____

_____

_____

_____

_____

_____

_____

_____

Mark 4:39 KJV

"And he arose, and rebuked the wind, and said unto the sea, Peace, be still. And the wind ceased, and there was a great calm."

Today's Prayer:

Dear Heavenly Father,

I'm so glad that you gave me the power and authority to speak to the winds, waves, and the sea and command that peace be still all around me and in me. At times, the storms of life may be raging all around me, but I know that I can speak to the storm and tell the storm to be still and remain quiet. Lord God, the calm and stillness that I will experience only comes from you and your presence. When there is a storm out on the horizon, the weather man looks for the eye of the storm and he reports that. The eye of the storm is the calmest and most peaceful place of that storm. God, show up in my storms of life and allow your calm and peacefulness to be present. Let your gift of peace be a prominent force in my life. I command that peace be still in every situation and circumstance in my life. God, I thank you for your spirit of peace and calmness. Amen.

_____

_____

_____

_____

_____

_____

Mark 5:34 AMP

"Then He said to her,"Daughter, your faith [your personal trust and confidence in Me] has restored you to health; go in peace and be [permanently] healed from your suffering."

Today's Prayer:

Lord God,

If my faith and personal trust and confidence in you, Lord Jesus, can make me whole and give me peace, I pray that over my life right now in Jesus Name. Faith and peace work together. I must have faith in order to have peace. Father God, give me mustard seed faith that will cause me, _____, [your name] to be healed through and through, from the inside out, and from the crown of my head to the soles of my feet. I call forth your healing power and your peace that will cause me to be permanently healed of every pain, disease, sickness, attitude, fear, worry, etc., in Jesus' Name. Amen.

_____

_____

_____

_____

_____

_____

_____

_____

Mark 9:50 NLT

"Salt is good for seasoning. But if it loses its flavor, how do you make it salty again? You must have the qualities of salt among yourselves and live in peace with each other."

Today's Prayer:

My God in Heaven,

Help me, _____, [your name] to display salt-like character in order to keep the qualities in me that will allow me to be seasoned, and don't allow me to lose my flavor. I know that food doesn't have any flavor and it doesn't taste good if it's not seasoned. I want my prayers to go up and be like a sweet smell to your nostril. I must maintain and exercise my peace and be peaceful with all. I need to be peaceful in my home, at church, in the store, on my job, in my town, in my city, and in my neighborhood. God help me to live in peace and be peaceful with all. Amen.

_____

_____

_____

_____

_____

_____

_____

_____

Luke 2:14 AMP

"Glory to God in the highest [heaven], And on earth peace among men with whom He is well-pleased."

Today's Prayer:

Dear God,

Thank you for your glory in the heavens and in the earth. I pray that you are well pleased with me, _____, [your name] so that I can take part in your unyielding promise of peace that I need and that I so desire. I need your peace in my mind; I need your peace in my spirit; and I need your peace in my heart. I also need your peace in every way. I want to share your peace with others so that they can experience this sweet peace that only you can give. I want to command peace to be still in the situations that are concerning me. I want to dispatch your peace in the places where I am not but you are everywhere and so is your peace. Thank you Father for your peace and that's peace like no other.

_____

_____

_____

_____

_____

_____

_____

Luke 10:5 NLT

"Whenever you enter someone's home, first say, 'May God's peace be on this house.'"

Today's Prayer:

Lord God,

Because of your peace that dwells within me, through me, and around me, I can declare peace in every home that I visit. Lord, let that same peace be in my home and in every individual who comes into my home. When your peace is present, it brings a sense of calm and tranquility. Yes, God, that is the peace that I want to continue to experience in my life and throughout my years. As I walk over the threshold of someone's home, let me declare and decree peace be on this house, and where your peace is your protection is there also. I thank you, God, for your peace and your protection. You have your own PPE that will protect me and my family from danger seen and unseen, and for that I say thank you. I can't thank you enough for your peace and protection.

Luke 10:6 AMP

"And if anyone of peace is there [someone who is sweet-spirited and hospitable], your [blessing of] peace will rest on him; but if not, it will return to you."

Today's Prayer:

Father God,

Thank you for your peace and the acknowledgment in knowing that your peace is upon me, _____, [your name] and wherever I am your peace will follow me. If your peace is not welcome, then I need to shake the dust off my feet and move on in order to maintain the peace of God and peace within. You are so awesome, and during the times of craziness your peace brings a solace and a peaceful atmosphere. Allow me to be sweet-spirited and hospitable so that I can inhabit your blessing of peace. Lord God, I thank you for your peace.

_____

_____

_____

_____

_____

_____

_____

_____

_____

Luke 14:32 TLB

"If the decision is negative, then while the enemy troops are still far away, he will send a truce team to discuss terms of peace."

Today's Prayer:

Lord God,

Sometimes I pray, and the decision that I'm waiting for is not a favorable one, and the enemy has sent his troops to come up against me, but you always give me a way out. You will send a team of peacemakers, intercessors, and encouragers to bring about a peaceful outcome and for that I say thank you. Nobody but you can bring the type of peace that allows me to rest in green pastures and restores my soul. You are gracious and kind, and you bring peace to every situation in every way. Thank you for your love and your peace, peace like no other. You Are My God, and You Are My Peace.

_____

_____

_____

_____

_____

_____

_____

_____

Luke 24:36 NLT

"And just as they were telling about it, Jesus himself was suddenly standing there among them. "Peace be with you," he said."

Today's Prayer:

Dear God,

Allow me, _____, [your name] to feel your presence and allow me to know that you are near in every situation and in every circumstance. Show up in my life and show up in all that I do. During the hardest moments of my life, I can always count on you to be there. You, God, have been my peace in the midst of my life's storms, tornadoes, tsunamis, hurricanes, earthquakes, and the various pandemics. When you show up, you bring peace like no other. God, you show up in that still small voice and say, "peace be with you" and "peace be still," and everything just changes. My life is forever changed and my situations are forever changed because of your peace. When peace steps up on the scene, everything is still and quiet. There is a calmness that comes over me because of your peace. Even when I hear bad news there is something about your peace; it puts me in a peaceful state. I can't explain the feeling nor can I understand it; all I know is that your peace shows up and is a prevalent force in my life. Thank you so much for your peace, peace like a river.

_____

_____

_____

_____

_____

_____

John 14:27 NLT

"I am leaving you with a gift—peace of mind and heart. And the peace I give is a gift the world cannot give. So don't be troubled or afraid."

Today's Prayer:

Lord God,

The many gifts that I have received from you are awesome and welcoming. I cherish each one, but there is nothing like your peace. Your gift of peace changes the atmosphere; your gift of peace changes decisions and gives me good guidance; your gift of peace changes my heart and my mind. There is nothing like your gift of peace. I am grateful for your gift of peace. I take time to unwrap your gift of peace every day and in every way. I take your gift of peace with me wherever I go. I don't keep your gift of peace to myself but I share it with everyone in every place. Peace is a gift and I am grateful to sow your spirit of peacefulness. Yes, God, I know now that I'm able to sow your peace and reap the harvest of peacefulness. Because of your gift of peace, I am not afraid, and anxiety can't rule in my life any longer; it can't even ride with me. It must be diminished from my life forever because of your peace. Thank you for your gift of peace in every way.

_____

_____

_____

_____

_____

_____

John 16:33 AMP

"I have told you these things, so that in Me you may have [perfect] peace. In the world you have tribulation and distress and suffering, but be courageous [be confident, be undaunted, be filled with joy]; I have overcome the world." [My conquest is accomplished, My victory abiding.]"

Today's Prayer:

Father God,

There is no peace in this world but I can have perfect peace in you. There is so much trouble, loneliness, isolation, distress, tears, death, sadness, loss, and grief, but in all of these situations that we deal with in our life, we can still find that perfect peace in you. I trust you, and I trust your word. I rely on your word to speak peace to me and through me. I have assurance in you and I can count on you not to fail me. You have always been by my side. I am in this world that is full of sorrow but you have overcome the world. I can still have joy in all that life brings because of your perfect peace. Your peace is with me, in me, under me, through me, and around me. You told me that I can have perfect peace and I receive it. Thank you, God, for your unfailing peace, peace that shows up when needed to bring calmness in the atmosphere. Your peace is like no other.

_____

_____

_____

_____

_____

John 20:19 NIV

"On the evening of that first day of the week, when the disciples were together, with the doors locked for fear of the Jewish leaders, Jesus came and stood among them and said, "Peace be with you!"

Today's Prayer:

Dear Jesus,

You're the center of my peace. You are great and mighty. You show up on the scene and everything changes. The atmosphere knows your presence and must honor and acknowledge you when you show up. In the midst of my hardest moments, when fear tries to grip me, you, Lord, will come and stand beside me. You tell me, "Peace be with you," and something changes within me and around me. I am secure in your peace. There is calm and tranquility that comes over me when your peace shows up. I am then confident that your peace is with me and in me. Your very presence brings perfect peace, the peace that many desire to have today. It is the peace that you can't buy but it's given out as a gift from God. Thank you for your peace that no one can fathom.

John 20:21 AMP

"Then Jesus said to them again, "Peace to you; as the Father has sent Me, I also send you [as My representatives].""

Today's Prayer:

Most Gracious and loving God,

You have given me, _____, [your name] the gift of your peace and for that I am grateful. You have allowed me to obtain and maintain your peace in every situation and circumstance. Now, I can represent you and the embodiment of your perfect peace. You have deployed me to places where peace was needed and when I showed up, I showed up with your peace. Peace, Peace, Peace there is nothing like the peace of God. You can't buy peace; you can't borrow peace; and you can't lend peace because it's a gift from God. Thank you for your precious gift of peacefulness.

_____

_____

_____

_____

_____

_____

_____

_____

Acts 10:36 AMP

"You know the message which He sent to the sons of Israel, announcing the good news of peace through Jesus Christ, who is Lord of all."

Today's Prayer:

Jesus Christ,

You are Lord of all. You have brought me good news with all the chaos and craziness that goes on in my life. This good news is I have peace through you. We can't obtain peace without you. You have been a prominent force in my life and for that I say thank you. I've matured in my walk with you and knowing that your word is true, I can accept your gift of peace. You said, "my peace I leave with you." I believe what I see when your peace is manifested in my life and around me. I can rest in knowing that there is good news of peace in you and through you. Thank you for your peace. It is your perfect peace.

Romans 1:7 AMP

"[I am writing] to all who are beloved of God in Rome, called to be saints (God's people) and set apart for a sanctified life, [that is, set apart for God and His purpose]: Grace to you and peace [inner calm and spiritual well-being] from God our Father and from the Lord Jesus Christ."

Today's Prayer:

Lord God,

Thank you for calling me into sanctification, a life that has been set apart for your purpose; you have graced me with your peace and for that I say thank you. It's that inner calmness and spiritual well-being that I need every day dealing with life itself. I am so very grateful that I know who you are and that I can trust your words. I depend on you to give me perfect peace in the midst of all that I go through. It's something about your peace that is obtainable for me and everyone else. I will embrace and accept your gift of peace. Thank you.

Romans 2:10 TLB

"But there will be glory and honor and peace from God for all who obey him, whether they are Jews or Gentiles."

Today's Prayer:

Dear God,

You have said in your word that there will be peace from you if I obey. Help me to fall in line with your word, listen, and do exactly what is said. Your peace means a lot to me, and I need your peace. I want to do all I can to maintain and cultivate your peace. It's my peace and I will protect the gift of peace that you so freely give. Thank you, God, for your peace that is indescribable.

_____

_____

_____

_____

_____

_____

_____

_____

_____

Romans 3:17 NLV

"They know nothing about peace."

Today's Prayer:

Father God,

Help me not to go down the path where I don't experience your peace or know what your peace looks like. Allow me to embrace your peace and feel the peace of God that passes my understanding. The feelings of restlessness are the feelings that I never want to be comfortable with. I want to feel your peace inside and out. It's your peace that will help me through life most challenging times. That's the peace I need, and that's the peace that I will embrace. How sad, and how lonely and unfortunate one must feel who have not experienced your peace. I pray for those today that they will accept your gift of peace and feel the peace of God in their life and in their situation. God, I thank you for your peace.

Romans 5:1 NLV

"Now that we have been made right with God by putting our trust in Him, we have peace with Him. It is because of what our Lord Jesus Christ did for us."

Today's Prayer:

God,

I put complete trust in you, and therefore you have given me peace. I have seen your great work, and it has caused me to trust in you. You are a miracle worker, and you do great things. Your peace that you give to me is just one of the great things that you do. I need your peace in everything that I do and in everything that I say. So much has happened in my life, and your peace is what I need to let me know that all is well. It's that tranquil space and calmness that is prevalent for me in this day and time. Thank you for your peace, peace like no other.

Romans 8:6 NLT

"So letting your sinful nature control your mind leads to death. But letting the Spirit control your mind leads to life and peace."

Today's Prayer:

Dear Heavenly Father,

Help me not to allow my flesh to control my mind that leads to death. Let your spirit control my life that leads to life and give me the peace that I need in my life. Your peace is so important and is needed in everything that I say and do. I am grateful to know you and to know that your peace is a life changer and can change everything around me and in me. Father God, I thank you for your peace in the midst of my circumstances.

Romans 10:15 KJV

"And how shall they preach, except they be sent? as it is written, How beautiful are the feet of them that preach the gospel of peace, and bring glad tidings of good things!"

Today's Prayer:

Lord God,

Send me, I'll go. I'll go wherever you want me to go to preach the good news of the gospel. I will share your word and the gospel of peace. I will share it with everyone in every place, at the grocery store, at WalMart, at Target, at the shopping mall, at church, at work, at the gas station, at the post office, in DMV, in the airport, on the plane, on Facebook, on social media, on Zoom, and on the prayer line, etc. Whenever and wherever the opportunity arises, I will share your message of peace. Thank you, God, because I want to go in the right direction where your peace is needed and bring the good news of the gospel of peace. I'm grateful that your peace brings me and others good news and tranquility. It is possible to actually have peace in this life and in your world but it's only attainable through God.

Romans 12:18 AMP

"If possible, as far as it depends on you, live at peace with everyone."

Today's Prayer:

Dear Heavenly Father,

I know today that my peace and being peaceful with others depends solely on me and no one else. Your word tells me, _____, [your name] to live at peace with everyone. I know that I may not hit the mark every time but I am striving for your perfect peace, that inner calm and spiritual well-being. God, my prayer today is that everywhere my feet tread allow your peace to accompany me in every place and in every way.

_____

_____

_____

_____

_____

_____

_____

_____

_____

Romans 14:17 TLB

"For, after all, the important thing for us as Christians is not what we eat or drink but stirring up goodness and peace and joy from the Holy Spirit."

Today's Prayer:

Thank you God,

For showing me that as a Christian it's not about just eating and drinking but it's about your goodness and your peace that comes with joy. Thank you for your Spirit that is in me, that is everywhere and in everyone. It's most important for me to have your gift of perfect peace because your peace will bring me goodness and joy. Peace brings calm and spiritual well-being to me and to the hearts and mind of others. God, your peace can change a whole nation. Your peace is a blessing to everyone. Thank you for allowing me to stir up your peace within and everywhere I go.

_____

_____

_____

_____

_____

_____

_____

_____

Romans 14:19 AMP

"So then, let us pursue [with enthusiasm] the things which make for peace and the building up of one another [things which lead to spiritual growth]."

Today's Prayer:

Lord God,

Your word brings me life and gladness. Your word awakens my spirit and causes me to seek it. I will pursue your inner peace with excitement and everything that makes for peace. I will build on peace; I will run after peace; I will cultivate peace; I will maintain my peace; and I will sow peace into the lives of others. I know how vital peace is and what it takes to keep my peace within. I honor and reverence your gift of peace. I will be so very careful not to allow anyone to take my peace away. I will stand watch over my peace and be watchful of those who are peace breakers because my peace is a treasure. I will build up others as it relates to being peaceful because this is part of being spiritually mature. Thank you, God, for your peace, peace that fills my soul.

_____

_____

_____

_____

_____

_____

_____

Romans 15:13 AMP

"May the God of hope fill you with all joy and peace in believing [through the experience of your faith] that by the power of the Holy Spirit you will abound in hope and overflow with confidence in His promises."

Today's Prayer:

Dear Most Holy and Gracious God,

There are so many promises in you and those still waiting to be fulfill not broken promises but kept promises. Thank you for filling me with your peace. There is peace through many experiences where faith is in operation. Peace comes over time with maturity and finally realizing and saying: Lord I need your peace. I know that your peace is a gift, but I have to accept the gift, unwrap it and use it. Holy God, your peace brings me hope, joy, and confidence in you. Thank you for your joy and your peace.

Romans 15:33 NLT

"And now may God, who gives us his peace, be with you all. Amen."

Today's Prayer:

Father God,

Thank you for your continued reminder about the peace that you give. I am grateful to be a partaker of your peace—peace like no other. I need you and I need your peace. I have no peace without you, I have no peace without prayer, and I have no peace if I don't accept the gift of your peace. So today I, _____, [your name] accept the gift of peace. I will nourish the gift of peace; I will feed it and I will uphold it. It's your peace and I won't take it for granted. I am thankful for your peace.

_____

_____

_____

_____

_____

_____

_____

_____

_____

_____

Romans 16:20 MSG

"Don't be gullible in regard to smooth-talking evil. Stay alert like this, and before you know it the God of peace will come down on Satan with both feet, stomping him into the dirt. Enjoy the best of Jesus!"

Today's Prayer:

Dear God,

I thank you for your peace and for being a peaceful God. You share your peace with others, and you help me to keep my peace. Yes, even when the enemy comes to try and take my peace away you want me to be watchful of those sly moves of restlessness. You have also reassured me that you will take care of the enemy. You will crush him with your feet in order for me to maintain my peacefulness. You want me to enjoy my life and the best of what your son, Jesus, has to offer me. Therefore, I have to trust that you will take down anything that comes against my peace. I am grateful that I can search your word and find more than 300 scriptures of hope in your peace.

_____

_____

_____

_____

_____

_____

_____

1 Corinthians 1:3 AMP

"Grace to you and peace [inner calm and spiritual well-being] from God our Father and the Lord Jesus Christ."

Today's Prayer:

Lord God,

I need your inner calm and spiritual well-being. I can't make it without your peace. Your peace brings an atmosphere of peacefulness when chaos is all around. I feel safe and secure in you because of the peace that you bring to me during every crisis in my life. Help me to rely on your peace in every situation. Peace represents you, God, because I have no peace without you, and I will not know peace without you. Allow me to know your ways and know you more and more so that I can experience your constant and consistent peace. God, I thank you for your perfect peace.

_____

_____

_____

_____

_____

_____

_____

_____

1 Corinthians 7:15 NLT

"But if the husband or wife who isn't a believer insists on leaving, let them go. In such cases the believing husband or wife is no longer bound to the other, for God has called you to live in peace."

Today's Prayer:

Heavenly Father,

Thank you for calling me into your peace and letting me know that no matter who leaves my life, I must let them go. You want me to have your peace and sometimes that means letting go of the people and things that causes chaos and distractions in my life. You have called me into a peaceful state of mind, a peaceful state of being and for that I say thank you. You let me know that I'm not spiritually or morally bound to the unbeliever because you have released me so that I can experience your perfect peace. It's your peace that brings me joy, hope, and confidence in you and your word. Oh God, I am grateful to have known your peace because it changes the way I feel and the way I think. I am releasing everyone and everything that disturbs my peaceful state of being. God, I thank you for calling me into your peace.

1 Corinthians 14:33 AMP

"For God [who is the source of their prophesying] is not *a God* of confusion *and* disorder but of peace *and* order."

Today's Prayer:

Heavenly Father,

Your word reminds me that you are a God of order and not disorder. You like harmony and you look for it as well. Help me to be the person whom you are looking for who brings order and peace to every situation and circumstance. I thank you for your peace and for filling me with peacefulness. Just like your love, I can share your peace with others. I strive after your peace every day. It is important in my life to have peace and to be peaceful. Although at times I see where the enemy tries to break my peace and my peaceful state of being, I must recognize his tactics and remain peaceful because you are not the one that brings the confusion. God, you are peace. I know that in this world that I live in I will have storms and tribulation but I can have your peace in the midst of it all. Thank you God for your wonderful and gracious peace that you give as a gift to me.

2 Corinthians 1:2 AMP

"Grace to you and peace [inner calm and spiritual well-being] from God our Father and the Lord Jesus Christ."

Today's Prayer:

God,

You keep saying throughout your word, grace and peace, inner calm and spiritual well-being. This should also be my salutation and greeting to others that I am coming in peace and that our connection is a peaceful one. Help me, Lord, to get peace down on the inside of me and let it be a part of me and let it be who I am. Being peaceful and a peace bearer is what I desire to attain. I will talk about peace and share peace with everyone. It is not my peace, but it's your peace that you give to me. Thank you, God, for your peace, peace that only you can give.

2 Corinthians 13:11 AMP

"Finally, believers, rejoice! Be made complete [be what you should be], be comforted, be like-minded, live in peace [enjoy the spiritual well-being experienced by believers who walk closely with God]; and the God of love and peace [the source of lovingkindness] will be with you."

Today's Prayer:

Dear Loving and Kind God,

Help me, _____, [your name] to walk closely with you and live in your peace. I want to enjoy your spiritual well-being as a believer. I want to be comforted, I want to have joy, and I want to be loved by you. I'm confident and I have complete trust in you and your word that if I live in peace, then you, the loving and kind God, will be with me. Thank you, God, for the reassurance that I have in your peace. The peace of God that I don't understand but it's your peace. Even though I don't understand your ways, I accept your peace.

_____

_____

_____

_____

_____

_____

_____

_____

Galatians 1:3 AMP

"Grace to you and peace [inner calm and spiritual well-being] from God our Father and the Lord Jesus Christ."

Today's Prayer:

Father God,

Again you have allowed me to see your salutation of a peace greeting. I want peace to be engrafted into my life and be a part of my everyday being. Your peace brings me solace and relieves me from the feeling of unrest that is going on all around me. Lord, let your peace grip me like a vise grip and be in me and around me. Lord God, so many are experiencing fear and anxiety, but allow your salutation of peace to become one with me. God, I want your peace greeting to be my greeting so that others can experience your gift of peace, be peaceful and share your peace. Thank you, God, for your loving kindness and your peace.

Galatians 5:22–23 TLB

"But when the Holy Spirit controls our lives he will produce this kind of fruit in us: love, joy, peace, patience, kindness, goodness, faithfulness, gentleness and self-control."

Today's Prayer:

Dear God,

I want the Holy Spirit to control my life so that it can produce the kind of peaceful fruit that brings along patience, kindness, goodness, faithfulness, gentleness and self-control. God, this empowers me to be at peace and be peaceful in all that I do because of the fruit that peace is associated with. I want to be a fruit bearer. Ah, God, there is something about peace that changes my life and the individual lives around me. Let me, _____, [your name] be a bearer of your peace, a peacemaker is what I want to be. I need you because there is no peace without you. Thank you for your peace.

_____

_____

_____

_____

_____

_____

_____

_____

Galatians 6:15-16 TLB

"What counts is whether we really have been changed into new and different people. May God's mercy and peace be upon all of you who live by this principle and upon those everywhere who are really God's own."

Today's Prayer:

Lord God,

Change my life and transform me into a new person, adopting and accepting your written principles and your mercy and your peace. God, I want you to change my heart, change my mind, and change everything about me so that your mercy and peace will be upon me and be everywhere I go. Your forgiveness is always there for me, and your compassion fails me not. I belong to you, and you are my God. Your peace is what I need to calm all the storms in my life. Lord help me, _____, to become an all-weather person being able to stay peaceful and calm in any storm. I thank you for your peace, peace like no other.

_____

_____

_____

_____

_____

_____

_____

Ephesians 1:2 AMP

"Grace to you and peace [inner calm and spiritual well-being] from God our Father and the Lord Jesus Christ."

Today's Prayer:

Dear Heavenly Father,

Each one of your salutations of grace and peace brings me great joy and understanding of the importance of sharing this greeting with others. I believe that this greeting can change everything that a person may be experiencing at that moment. I need your good posture and inner calm and spiritual well-being every day and in every way. It is your grace and peace that only comes from God. Your peace defines me and your peace builds my character. Father God, I thank you for your grace and peace.

_____

_____

_____

_____

_____

_____

_____

_____

_____

Ephesians 2:14 NLV

"We have peace because of Christ. He has made the Jews and those who are not Jews one people. He broke down the wall that divided them."

Today's Prayer:

Wonderful Savior Jesus Christ,

First of all, I thank you because there is no division in you. You broke down the walls that divided us so that we can become one people and live in your peace. You made it possible for us to have peace. You have made us one, and we should be able to get along with each other and live in peace. You broke down the walls that would divide us, and you made us peaceful amongst each other. Yes, God, I know it's possible for us to obtain peace and maintain your peace. I am grateful that I have your peace. I may not hit the mark every day as it concerns peace, but I will continue to strive after peace and live in a state of peacefulness. God, I need your peace that brings me into a peaceful state of mind. I'm thankful for your peace, peace like no other. Lord, it is your peace that gives me inner calmness and tranquility.

Ephesians 2:17 NLV

"Then Christ came and preached the Good News of peace to you who were far away from God. And He preached it to us who were near God."

Today's Prayer:

Dear God,

I thank you for coming into my life at such a pivotal time and in the right space when needed. I thank you for advocating for me and preaching your peace. Your peace transcends everything in my life and every circumstance. Your peace has transformed my whole entire life and everything that I do. I will never be the same again because of your peace. I appreciate your gift of peacefulness, that inner calm and tranquil state of mind and being. Because of your peace that rules in my heart, mind, and soul, my life will forever be changed. God it is your peace that is with me, _____, [your name] whether I'm near or far from you. Yes, God, I'm reminded that I may not be on point or hit the mark everyday concerning my gift of peace that you have given to me but I know that it is with me. All I need to do is take ownership of my peace, maintain my peace, and let it operate in my life. I need to let your peace fill the atmosphere where chaos has erupted. Your peace calms any and all raging storms of life. Your peace is a storm catcher. Where peace is, calm is also present. I thank you, God, for your perfect peace.

_____

_____

_____

_____

_____

Ephesians 4:3 AMP

"Make every effort to keep the oneness of the Spirit in the bond of peace [each individual working together to make the whole successful]."

Today's Prayer:

Heavenly Father,

Today and every day I will make every attempt to keep the bond of peace as I work with others. It's your peace that brings unity to all that I endeavor to do, but if there is no peace amongst us there is no oneness and there is no success. So God help me, _____, [your name] to keep the oneness of the Spirit in the bond of peace. Allow me to work together with others in order to manifest a peaceful and successful outcome. Your gift of peace can reassure me that everything will be well even if I don't hear it, see it, or feel it. It is your peace that changes the trajectory of my life, my situations, and circumstances. I will hold on and grip your peace like a warm blanket on a chilly night. Your peace is my comfort and my tranquility. I thank you, Father God, for your peace that brings me joy and happiness.

_____

_____

_____

_____

_____

_____

_____

Ephesians 6:15 AMP

"And having strapped on your feet the gospel of peace in preparation [to face the enemy with firm-footed stability and the readiness produced by the good news]."

Today's Prayer:

My Lord, My God,

Help me to strap on my feet the gospel of peace to help me, _____, [your name] face all that the enemy has set before me with a firm foot and stability and with readiness of the good news that is the good news of the gospel of peace. Your peace produces good news, and it is shared abroad in the lives of so many. Your peace is also in every situation that we face. I'm grateful for your peace that assists me, _____, [your name] in the face of adversity. I can pull on your strength and your peace when I need to in every way, every day and wherever I go. Your peace can be in me, through me, over me, and around me. It is your peace that our world needs and that I need when times call for peace. Let me orchestrate and facilitate your peacefulness in all that I do. I thank you for the grace that gives me peace that can only come from you, God.

_____

_____

_____

_____

_____

_____

Ephesians 6:23 NLT

"Peace be with you, dear brothers and sisters, and may God the Father and the Lord Jesus Christ give you love with faithfulness."

Today's Prayer:

Oh God,

How I thank you for your peace being with me, in me, and through me. Your peace surrounds me, and in the storms of life I have peace like no other. Thank you for your love and faithfulness that you have toward me. You have always been there for me, and your peace has taken over the situations that were unbearable at times. During some of the hardest times in my life, you have been there and for that I say thank you. Your peace is what I need to calm the raging seas in my life. There is nothing like your peace and your peacefulness. Thank you for allowing your peace to surround me and walk alongside of me. No matter what I face I will always look toward your peace. Thank you, God, for a peaceful state of mind.

Philippians 1:2 AMP

"Grace to you and peace [inner calm and spiritual well-being] from God our Father and the Lord Jesus Christ."

Today's Prayer:

Lord God,

I thank you for the reassurance concerning your peace, your inner calm and spiritual well-being that only comes from you, Father God. This scripture is placed throughout the Bible in the New Testament as a constant reminder of this salutation. Allow me to address others in this manner in order to bring peace, inner calm and spiritual well-being to someone else's life. Lord God, please help me to be sensitive to those who are going through the storms of life and need peace. Your peace has rescued my life, and I will never be the same. Your peace is a constant reminder that you are with me everywhere I go and in every situation that I have to face. I will be peaceful in my mind, in my heart and in my spirit. Allow me to introduce others to the peace of God that surpasses all of my understanding. Your peace is like no other. Thank you for your peace.

Philippians 4:7 AMP

"And the peace of God [that peace which reassures the heart, that peace] which transcends all understanding, [that peace which] stands guard over your hearts and your minds in Christ Jesus [is yours]."

Today's Prayer:

Dear Great and Holy One,

You have given me one of your most treasured gifts and that is your peace. Your peace is beyond anyone's understanding. Thank you for peace that reassures the heart and exceeded everything that I can imagine. I can't make it without your peace. Your peace stands watch and guard over my heart and my mind. So that even in the toughest season of my life your peace is always with me. When my heart is overwhelmed and my eyes are filled with tears, your peace is standing as a protector over my heart and mind. Your peace mends broken and sad hearts. Your peace keeps me clothed in my right mind. It's your peace that is with me, your peace is in me, and your peace is around me. I will maintain my peace at all costs. I will not let others take my peace. My peace is you, God. The Bible and others call it peace but I call peace you, God. You are my peace. Your peace goes with me everywhere I go. Let your peace spill over and go with me everywhere my feet go. I thank you, God, for your peace that is with me and in me.

_____

_____

_____

_____

_____

_____

Philippians 4:9 AMP

"The things which you have learned and received and heard and seen in me, practice these things [in daily life], and the God [who is the source] of peace *and* well-being will be with you."

Today's Prayer:

Ah God,

I was created in your image and after your likeness. I am to mirror everything that you are in my daily life. I have learned so much from you and I am still learning everyday about your ways. I have received guidance from you about my character and about the way I am to conduct myself. Your word is a constant reminder of the lifestyle that I am to practice and live and your word tells me that after during all of these things the God who is the source of all my peace and well-being will be with me. God, you are so good and you are so great. There is none like you. No one else can touch my heart and bring me peace like you can. Your word brings life, clarity, and peace in every situation that I have to face. I bless you in so many ways. I tell others about you because of your peace and well-being that only comes from you. I thank you today for your peace. I stand amazed at the peace that you have given to me in the midst of every crisis, circumstance, and storms of life. God, you are that peace. You come on the scene and it is a peace, be still moment. I thank you for your peace.

_____

_____

_____

_____

_____

_____

Colossians 1:2 AMP

"To the saints and faithful believers in Christ [who are] at Colossae: Grace to you and peace [inner calm and spiritual well-being] from God our Father."

Today's Prayer:

Thank You God,

Again I see this awesome salutation that brings your gift of peace to so many. I am so grateful for your inner calm and spiritual well-being that can only come from you. I can't make it without your peace. I need your peace in every area of my life. Help me, _____, [your name] to continue in your peace and in a peaceful state of mind. Thank you for your purposed peace that flows through me and brings peace to everyone I encounter. Thank you for allowing me to magnify your peace, yes, to make your peace bigger than any one of my situations and issues. It is your peace that can change a condition, a sickness, a circumstance, a state of affairs, relationships, vents, incidents, and accidents. Even if things don't go the way that I want them to go, your peace gives me the reassurances that I need that you are with me, every step of the way. Ah God (breathing in and out), I thank you for your peace.

_____

_____

_____

_____

_____

_____

_____

Colossians 1:20 NLV

"Everything in heaven and on earth can come to God because of Christ's death on the cross. Christ's blood has made peace."

Today's Prayer:

Thank You Jesus,

I thank you for your death on the cross and for your bloodshed that brought me peace! I thank you for giving me, _____, [your name] the drive and the desire to chase after your peace. I chase after your peace because your peace exceeds my thoughts and understanding of how peaceful I can be in the midst of the turbulence in my life. Your peace sustains me, your peace brings me joy and happiness, and your peace puts me in a peaceful state of mine. It is your peace; no one can give me peace but you, Father God. I can't be without your peace. It is important for me to live in peace and to be a carrier of your peace. Yes, God, I, _____, [your name] thank you for your peace, peace like no other.

Colossians 3:15 AMP

"Let the peace of Christ [the inner calm of one who walks daily with Him] be the controlling factor in your hearts [deciding and settling questions that arise]. To this peace indeed you were called as members in one body [of believers]. And be thankful [to God always]."

Today's Prayer:

Father God,

There are so many names that describe who you are to me and others, but today I need you to be my Father, my Papa. I need you in so many ways and right now I need your peace to be a stable force in my life. In this world I will have tribulations, tests, and trials, but your peace can make a difference in the outcome for me, _____, [your name]. It could be craziness all around me, but your peace brings peacefulness during those critical times. I thank you for your peace, that stable force that changes everything around me, under me, in me, and through me. Allow your peace to be a controlling factor in my heart, even when my heart is inundated with the cares of life. When my heart is overwhelmed, lead me to your perfect peace that will calm down each beat. When there are so many unanswered questions it is your peace that I am grateful for. I was called into your peace. You told me in your word that my peace I leave with you. Thank you, Papa, for your gift of constant peace in my life. It is your peace that I embrace in my life right now.

_____

_____

_____

_____

_____

1 Thessalonians 1:1 AMP

Thanksgiving for These Believers

"To the church of the Thessalonians in God the Father and the Lord Jesus Christ: Grace to you and peace [inner calm and spiritual well-being from God]."

Today's Prayer:

Most Gracious and Loving God,

Thank you once again for this salutation that brings me, _____, [your name] into a space of inner calm and spiritual well-being that only comes from you. Your peace that flows through me like a river is the tranquility and solace that I need in the midst of life's turbulence. I remember a time when I was flying in an airplane and we hit turbulence: the pilot came over the intercom and said we need to go up higher. When we reached a certain altitude, we were able to fly without the turbulence. Lord, help me to go higher in you where life's turbulence will not be effective because of your peace. Your peace is my serenity when my heart is heavy, when my mind is full of worry, and when my spirit is down. It is your peace, peace like no other. I can't make it without your peace and inner calm. Help me, Lord, to grab a hold of your peace when life has disappointed me and I've been dealt the wrong card. Let your peace take me to a place of acceptance knowing that all will be well because you are my perfect peace. Thank you Father, for your peace that surrounds me and that is in me.

_____

_____

_____

_____

_____

I Thessalonians 5:12–13 AMP

Christian Conduct

"Now we ask you, brothers and sisters, to appreciate those who diligently work among you [recognize, acknowledge, and respect your leaders], who are in charge over you in the Lord and who give you instruction, and [we ask that you appreciate them and] hold them in the highest esteem in love because of their work [on your behalf]. Live in peace with one another."

Today's Prayer:

Dear God,

Help me, _____, [your name] to live in peace with others even if they are not peaceful. I want to remain in a peaceful state of mind no matter what the atmosphere feels like and what the atmosphere appears to be. I don't have to allow other individuals' fear, anxiety, restlessness, anger, and personal and emotional situations to get in the way of my peace. My peace belongs to me and I will maintain it and take ownership of it. Because it is my peace, no one else has control over it but me. Lord God, please allow me to cultivate my peace and be in a peaceful state in the presence of others and in the worse situations that I have to encounter. I thank you, God, for the gift of peace; your perfect peace that you give to me, I accept.

_____

_____

_____

_____

_____

1 Thessalonians 5:23 AMP

"Now may the God of peace Himself sanctify you through and through [that is, separate you from profane and vulgar things, make you pure and whole and undamaged—consecrated to Him—set apart for His purpose]; and may your spirit and soul and body be kept complete and [be found] blameless at the coming of our Lord Jesus Christ."

Today's Prayer:

My God,

I know that everything you represent is peaceful. You are the epitome of peace, and you stand in every place where peace is needed. Your peace surrounds me and covers me. Your peace sets me apart from the rest. Your peace completes every cycle in my life. I can live in peace because of you. I don't care what I see, I don't care what others say, I don't care about what I hear or what goes on around me; it is your peace that will rule in my life in every place and in everything that I have to face. When the phone rings in the middle of the night and it's not the news you want to hear, it is your peace that brings calm and peacefulness over me. I thank you so much, God, for being that force of peace and protection that I, _____, [your name] need every day and in every way.

_____

_____

_____

_____

_____

_____

II Thessalonians 1:2 AMP

"Grace to you and peace [inner calm and spiritual well-being] from God the Father and the Lord Jesus Christ."

Today's Prayer:

Once Again, God,

We are faced with one of your awesome salutations of grace and peace. Lord God, today I thank you for your inner quietness and tranquility when chaos has erupted all around me, and my mind is full of thoughts that cause me to fear. Your peace and spiritual well-being bring me comfort and security. Fear can't stand in the midst of your peace. I so appreciate your peace that consoles and reassures me, _____, [your name] that you have it all in control. I need to allow your peace to rest, rule, and abide in my life. Yes, it is your peace that passes all my understanding. It is incredible; although I will never understand your peace, it still belongs to me, and I receive and acknowledge your peace gift of peace. Thank you, God, for your gift of peace; peace like no other, it is mine. I take full responsibility for my peace. I own it. I am watchful for peace breakers. You will not disturb my gift of peace and not distract my peace. I will let the peace of God win in me and around me.

_____

_____

_____

_____

_____

_____

2 Thessalonians 3:16 AMP

"Now may the Lord of peace Himself grant you His peace at all times and in every way [that peace and spiritual well-being that comes to those who walk with Him, regardless of life's circumstances]. The Lord be with you all."

Today's Prayer:

Lord,

Right now you have endowed me, _____, [your name] with your peace; it is your peace at all times in every way possible. God, as I walk with you, your word tells me that your peace and tranquility will be mine regardless of life's circumstances. I trust all that your word says. I live by your word, and your word brings me joy, peace, and life. I'm happy to walk alongside of you knowing that I can obtain your peace and all of your promises. You have given me full access to your peace, and now I can obtain peace, peace like no other. As I continue to walk with you, I will take joy and pleasure in your peace. I just want to say, thank you, God, for granting me, _____, [your name] your peace at all times and every way.

_____

_____

_____

_____

_____

_____

_____

1 Timothy 1:2 NLT

"I am writing to Timothy, my true son in the faith. May God the Father and Christ Jesus our Lord give you grace, mercy, and peace."

Today's Prayer:

Dear Father God,

As Paul wrote to Timothy, his true son, he asked that you give him grace, mercy, and peace. I am asking for that as well for me and for my family. I pray that your grace, mercy, and peace be upon me, God. You are the one who gives out the abundance of all that I ask for. I need your peace in my life in every way and in every place. It is your peace that sets the atmosphere everywhere I go. It is your peace that changes my mindset and causes my heart to be at ease. It is your peace that rules in my heart and in my situations. Your peace that I need in every place that I step foot on will be mine; I decree it now. I thank you so much for your peace.

2 Timothy 2:22 AMP

"Run away from youthful lusts—pursue righteousness, faith, love, and peace with those [believers] who call on the Lord out of a pure heart."

Today's Prayer:

Lord God,

I will flee from every one of my feelings and desires that doesn't please you. Lord, out of a pure heart, I will pursue your righteousness, faith, love, and peace with those who call you Lord. I will spread your peace with everyone whom I come in contact with, no matter where I go. If I'm at the bank, at the grocery store, at the mall, at work, or at home, I will distribute and express your peace wherever my feet tread. It's your peace that brings me, _____, [your name] the faith and love that I need in every situation that I have to face. I believe that your name is called peace, although we call you God, you are peace. I believe that your name is also called love, joy, and faith; although we call you God you represent many other attributes. Your peace is what I desire to obtain in my life. God, you are my peace and I thank you for the peace that only you give.

_____

_____

_____

_____

_____

_____

_____

Titus 1:4 NLV

"I am writing to you, Titus. You are my true son in the faith which we both have. May you have loving-favor and peace from God the Father and Jesus Christ, the One Who saves."

Today's Prayer:

You Are the Most High God,

As Paul prayed for Titus and wrote to him, I, too, pray that I am your true son/daughter and I pray that your loving-favor and peace be upon me, _____, [your name] that peace that only comes from you and through you. And for that I say thank you; yes, I thank you for being my God and for being my peace. You are the epitome of what peace looks like and what peace feels like. There is no peace without you. So I partner with you and your perfect peace that keeps me sane and in a peaceful state of mind. Your peace, God, has become a stable force in my life. I don't care what life brings, who says what, and how the enemy uses individuals to try and destroy my peace; it won't work because you are my peace and you stabilize those areas in my life so my peace doesn't get destroyed. My peace will not be moved or shattered by anybody; it is my peace, and I take ownership of my peace. I accept the gift of your perfect peace. I will cherish your gift and maintain it. Thank you for the peacefulness that is in me, through me, under me, and around me.

_____

_____

_____

_____

_____

Philemon 1:3 AMP

"Grace to you and peace [inner calm and spiritual well-being] from God our Father and the Lord Jesus Christ."

Today's Prayer:

Lord God,

Your continued salutation throughout the word of God brings me, _____, [your name] into a space and time of inner calm and spiritual well-being that only comes from you, Father. My God, it is your peace that is prevalent and reigns in my life today and always. I know that if fear, anxiety, and worry try to creep upon me, I can always tap into your peace. Ah (breathe in and out), yes, the peace of God that you give, it is mine. It belongs to me. You gave me your perfect peace as a gift, but I must unwrap it and use it. Your peace is not a gift that can be put away on a shelf and be brought down at a convenient time. No, I must use the gift of peace every minute of the day because of the world I live in. This world is full of trouble and restlessness. The ultimate goal of the enemy is to destroy my peace, but the gift of God's peace is always with me and in me. Lord God you are the gift of peace. You are what peace looks like. God, I thank you for your peace, peace like a river flowing in me, around me, and through me.

_____

_____

_____

_____

_____

_____

Hebrews 11:31 KJV

"By faith the harlot Rahab perished not with them that believed not, when she had received the spies with peace."

Today's Prayer:

Dear God,

Help me to become like the harlot Rahab in a symbolic way concerning your peace. She removed fear and completed her God-given assignment. It's by faith that I am able to exercise my peace and receive those things and people you put in my path. My faith and peace will work together to do all that I am required to do, in and out season. My peace will be very pivotal in everything that I do concerning each assignment that you give to me. My peace is vital to the call and purpose that is upon my life. I'm grateful for your peace, peace like no other, the peace that will allow me to receive those whom I know and strangers whom I don't know. I read, Hebrews 13:2 (KJV), that I must be careful in those certain encounters because I may be entertaining angels unaware I thank you for your peace, Father God, that will transform the life of those that I visit, support, talk with, and fellowship with; it is your peace.

Hebrews 12:14 AMP

"Continually pursue peace with everyone, and the sanctification without which no one will [ever] see the Lord."

Today's Prayer:

Father God,

Allow me to be in continued peace with you and everyone around me. In all that I do, in all that I say, in all that I am, and how I live, I must chase after your peace because it's your peace that will allow me to see you and be in right standing with you. I must realize that others may be in a place of restlessness and may also be in a chaotic state of mind but that is not for me to judge or figure out. As for me, _____, [your name] I must be peaceful in every way and every time. It doesn't seem fair at times that I must stay peaceful, but if I am going to bring glory to the Father, I must hold on and gravitate to peace. It is beneficial to me that I cultivate and stay in a peaceful place so that I can be deployed to the place where peace is needed. Also my peace will help me in every way in my life. You called me into your peace. You said let the peace of God rule in my heart and mind and that is where I want your peace. Ah (breathe in and out) God, I can't shake your peace because I need your peace in my life to deal with life circumstances and when the storms are heavily raging all around me. Your peace will keep me calm and quiet. I bless you, God, for your peace, the peace that no one understands or peace that no one can fathom. I am in a good place because of your peace. I thank you, God, today and always, for your peacefulness that comes upon me when my heart is overwhelmed.

_____

_____

_____

_____

_____

Hebrews 13:20–21 AMP

"Now may the God of peace [the source of serenity and spiritual well-being] who brought up from the dead our Lord Jesus, the great Shepherd of the sheep, through the blood that sealed and ratified the eternal covenant, equip you with every good thing to carry out His will and strengthen you [making you complete and perfect as you ought to be], accomplishing in us that which is pleasing in His sight, through Jesus Christ, to whom be the glory forever and ever. Amen."

Today's Prayer:

Most Holy and Gracious God,

I thank you for your peace; you are the source of my serenity, tranquility, and spiritual well-being. You raised Jesus Christ from the dead and you gave me an eternal covenant through his bloodshed. You have given me every good thing that will assist me to complete each assignment that you will give to me. You are gracious and kind, and your peace gives me all the strength that I need to accomplish those things that please you and that will bring you glory. Father God, you have laid out the plan that encourages me, _____, [your name] to keep going in the midst of life's raging storms. I have everything that I need, and for that I'm grateful. It is your peace that rallies around me, that calms me, that soothes me, and that gives to me the tranquility that I need in those restless moments. It is your peace that gives me reassurance that you are present. I thank you, Father, for your peace that is always with me.

_____

_____

_____

_____

_____

James 3:18 AMP

"And the seed whose fruit is righteousness (spiritual maturity) is sown in peace by those who make peace [by actively encouraging goodwill between individuals]."

Today's Prayer:

Dear God,

I want to continue to sow good seed, especially the seeds of righteousness and peace; I will continue to sow the seed of peacefulness. I will walk in peace, I will talk peace, and I will celebrate your peacefulness. Everywhere my foot treads, I will leave a fragrance of your peace. You said peace I leave with you. I will hold on to your gift of peace and sow it into the lives of others. I will blow a fresh wind of peace. I will encourage those who are at war with others and with themselves. God, it is your peace that I will make between me and other individuals. Father God, you have supplied me with everything that I need to help me, _____, [your name] in the midst of all that I have to endure. When the storms of life are raging all around me, in every place you have given me your peace that brings quietness and allows me to be in a calm place. You are my peace. You are in the middle of every storm; you are the eye of the storm that is watching over me. God, I thank you for being my all and all and for being my peace.

_____

_____

_____

_____

_____

1 Peter 1:2 AMP

"According to the foreknowledge of God the Father by the sanctifying work of the Spirit to be obedient to Jesus Christ and to be sprinkled with His blood: May grace and peace [that special sense of spiritual well-being] be yours in increasing abundance [as you walk closely with God]."

Today's Prayer:

Dear God,

As I walk closely with you, allow your increasing abundance of peace to be with me, _____, [your name] in all that I do, in all that I say, and in everywhere I go. Let your special sense of spiritual well-being be mine in Jesus' Name. It's your grace and peace that I need every day and in every way. I am grateful that I am able to experience your peace in my everyday life. Your peace makes me happy and brings me so much joy. Even in the midst of life's crises, your peace is with me. I can rest in your peace because I know that you are my peace and you are my God. It's your peace that brings me into a place of tranquility and inner calmness. It's your peace that causes me to have joy and causes me to laugh during the storms of life. God, I thank you for your peace, peace like no other. Peace that I don't understand, your peace that causes me to be at peace with those who war against me. It's your peace, God, that allows me to keep moving when I want to stop. Thank you, God, for the peace that surpasses my understanding, it is your peace and it is a gift to me.

_____

_____

_____

_____

_____

1 Peter 3:11 AMP

"He must turn away from wickedness and do what is right. He must search for peace [with God, with self, with others] and pursue it eagerly [actively—not merely desiring it]."

Today's Prayer:

God,

You are peaceful and you want me, _____, [your name] to search for your peace and pursue it actively. I must desire your peace as well. Even in the midst of the most difficult seasons in my life, I must search for your peace; even when things are so chaotic I must actively pursue your peace. When the storms of life are raging everywhere I turn, I must desire your peace. I must be in a peaceful state of mind in all that I say and in all that I do. Help me to turn away from evil and do what is right by searching out and pursuing your peace. Yes, God it is something about your peace. I can't explain it but your peace calms everything in me, through me and around me. Your peace makes me feel at ease when life is making so much noise and I don't know which way to turn. It is your peace that lessens the noises that I hear and are trying to make me stop moving. Your peace brings with it a sense of calm and tranquility. I thank you, God, for your peace that I will decree over my life and over my situations. I will search for your peace, that is peace with God, peace with myself, and peace with others. I will actively continue to pursue your peace. I will desire to be at peace in all that I say and in all that I do. Thank you, God, for your wonderful and sound peace.

_____

_____

_____

_____

_____

1 Peter 5:14 AMP

"Greet one another with a kiss of love. To all of you who are in Christ, may there be peace."

Today's Prayer:

Most Gracious and Holy God,

Let there be peace within me, _____ , [your name] and through me no matter what I am facing. If those whom I am around are not peaceful, allow your peace to rest upon me. It is your peace that makes a difference in my life. Let your peace be with me everywhere I go. Allow worry and fear to cease within me because your peace is present. Your peace causes my whole life to be different and brings me into a state of peacefulness. It is that tranquil space and time that are critical when life is turned upside down. It is your peace that steps right on in at the most crucial time. Your peace lets me know that everything will be OK because you are with me. Your peace is the place I want to be, no matter what is going on in my life. I declare and decree your peace over me, in me, and through me right now in Jesus' Name. And it is so; your peace is what I am calling forth right now in my life and in my situation. It may look crazy right now, but your peace will make a difference in all that I face. Thank you, Daddy God, for your peace, peace like no other. It is your peace that the whole world needs right in this very moment.

_____

_____

_____

_____

_____

2 Peter 1:2 AMP

"Grace and peace [that special sense of spiritual well-being] be multiplied to you in the [true, intimate] knowledge of God and of Jesus our Lord."

Today's Prayer:

Father God,

Because I know who you are and I know that you are the author and finisher of my peace, it is possible to have a special sense of spiritual well-being that only comes from you. Your peace brings me into a space of intimacy with you. It is your peace and that inner calm that are like nothing that I have ever experienced before. It is your peace that changes my world around me and changes the atmosphere that I am in. Your peace allows my words to come out in a peaceful manner where others can have an encounter with your peace. It is the peace of God that is multiplied in my life. I may be in my own personal valley some days or I may be on the mountain top but it is your peace that I will meet and connect with everywhere I go and in all that I do and in all that I say. As I live my life, let your peace increase in me every minute of the day. Papa, I thank you for your peace, that peace that draws me closer to you. Let your peace flow through me and out of my life like a waterfall.

2 Peter 3:13–14 AMP

"But in accordance with His promise we expectantly await new heavens and a new earth, in which righteousness dwells. So, beloved, since you are looking forward to these things, be diligent and make every effort to be found by Him [at His return] spotless and blameless, in peace [that is, inwardly calm with a sense of spiritual well-being and confidence, having lived a life of obedience to Him]."

Today's Prayer:

My Lord and Savior Jesus Christ,

I am not perfect but I am striving for perfection. I am conscientious in every way to be found in you spotless and blameless in your peace, that inner calm, spiritual well-being, and confidence. I am grateful that you have called me your beloved and I am grateful for your promises that I hold onto with all my heart, mind, and soul. As for me, _____, [your name] I hold dear to your peace; your perfect peace is mines in all I do and say. It's your peace that gives me everything that I need in the midst of life's turmoil. I can't make it in this world and in the work that I do without your peace. I live in your peace, I walk in your peace, I speak in your peace, I see in your peace, and I hear in your peace. Father God, my life will be about your peace because you are my peace. I thank you so much for the peace of God, peace like no other. It is your peace, God, that runs in me, through me, under me, and around me. The peace of God is the peace that only you can give.

_____

_____

_____

_____

_____

2 John 1:3 AMP

"Grace, mercy, and peace (inner calm, a sense of spiritual well-being) will be with us, from God the Father and from Jesus Christ, the Father's Son, in truth and love."

Today's Prayer:

Thank you God,

Once again I am faced with your awesome peace salutation that I can share with so many who are in need of your perfect peace. I need your inner calm and spiritual well-being every day and in every way. Lord God, it is your peace that I need in this life, while dealing with these pandemics. I am not only dealing with the Covid-19 pandemic, but I am also dealing with my own personal life's pandemics and everything that comes with them. There are pandemics in my own life that I am facing and dealing with, but it is your peace that gives me what I need to continue moving forward toward my destiny. It is your peace that makes life possible; in all that I do and everywhere I go, your peace is there to assist me. Thank you for your peace, God, peace like other.

Jude 1:2 AMP

"May mercy and peace and love be multiplied to you [filling your heart with the spiritual well-being and serenity experienced by those who walk closely with God]."

Today's Prayer:

Lord God,

May your peace, be multiplied to me, _____, [your name] and may your peace fill my heart with the spiritual well-being and peacefulness that is only experienced by those who walk closely with you. Ah (breathe in and out), God, allow me to activate your peace so that I can apply peace to my everyday life and in each of my circumstances. I want my life to be pleasing to you, and I want my walk with you to be deeper and more meaningful than ever before. The seasons and times that we are living in today require me to live in your peace. There is chaos all around, there are life uncertainties, there is death, loss, and grief that we are face with every day, and there is fear, anxiety and worry, but there is peace in me and around me. It is your peace that surpasses all of my understanding. I thank you, God, for your peace; it is your peace that I rely on every minute of my day and in every way. Your peace keeps me sane and in a good place. Let me introduce peace to others.

_____

_____

_____

_____

_____

_____

Revelations 1:4 AMP

"Grace [be granted] to you and peace [inner calm and spiritual well-being], from Him Who is [existing forever] and Who was [continually existing in the past] and Who is to come."

Today's Prayer:

Lord Jesus,

I can depend on your peace that inner calm and spiritual well-being that will be with me, _____, [your name] forever. You are the peace of the past, the future, and forever. It is your peace that will change this whole world and change my life as well. Through life situations and circumstances I have learned to rely on and activate my peace. Peace changes the atmosphere, and it changes the way I think. I am grateful for the peace that I have experienced during life's pandemics and pandemoniums. I've known about peace for many years, but during Covid-19 shutdowns, isolation, sadness, tears, death, loss, and grief, I now see peace in a different way. Peace has a new look, feel, and sound. Peace removes fear, worry, and anxiety. I can now live in your perfect peace, no matter what is taken place around me. God, it is your peace that I am so honored and grateful to experience. Father God, I thank you for your peace, peace like no other, peace that only you give to those who walk closely with you. It Is Your Gift Of Peace That Keeps My Heart, Mind, And Soul In Christ Jesus. It Is Your Perfect Peace That Dwells In Me, Through Me, And Around Me.

_____

_____

_____

_____

_____

Special Thanks

Dear God, who is the head of my life and orders my steps, I must say 'thank you' over and over again because your works are great and abundant in my life. It has been your peace, the peace that passes all understanding that has continuously guided me throughout this journey called 'life'. God without You, and Your hand on my life, this would have not been possible. You have given me your covenant of peace during the most difficult times in my life. Peace, your wonderful, amazing and unfailing peace that has kept me, my heart and my mind throughout the years. It has been your ordered steps that have allowed me to keep going and moving toward my destiny. It's the peace of God that has given me the example to live a life of serenity in Christ Jesus. Because you are my peace, I can bring peace to others.

To Releasing the Word International Intercessory Prayer Partners (RWIIP), for believing in me and in the ministry that God has given to me. You have supported me in more ways than I can list. You all stepped in and assisted when needed and gave me your gift of 'yes' when asked if you would pray or minister the word of God. You all continue to support this ministry throughout the many events thus far and for that I say 'thank you' from the bottom of my heart. I pray that the peace of God be with each and every one of you and that God's peace be in you and around you. I pray that you guard your peace at all times, and that God deploys you to the places where peace is needed. And as God guides you to places that need peace, I pray that you will leave it in your passing through - as a lingering fragrance would linger behind.
Wake Up Your Day with Peace!

As I continue on my peace journey, I see that I am faced with various situations that I had never had to face in my life but I will "Keep Fighting the Good Fight of Peace" in every way and every day. Peace, Peace, Wonderful Peace. The peace that only comes from God will be forever mines and I pray it be yours as well.

Contact releasingtheword17@yahoo.com for prayer times and days of the week.

Made in the USA
Middletown, DE
18 March 2022

62719489R00128